Messing Around with
WATER PUMPS AND SIPHONS
A Children's Museum
Activity Book

Messing Around with WATER PUMPS AND SIPHONS
A Children's Museum Activity Book

by Bernie Zubrowski

Illustrated by Steve Lindblom

Little, Brown and Company
Boston   Toronto   London

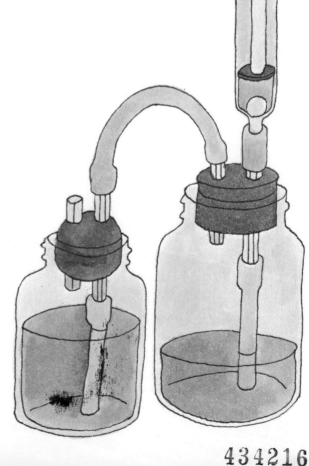

Library of Congress Cataloging in Publication Data

Zubrowski, Bernie.
  Messing around with water pumps and siphons.

  (A Children's Museum activity book)
  SUMMARY: Explains the principles of suction and
compression and includes directions for construct-
ing simple and complex water devices and for using
them in experiments and demonstrations.
    1. Pumping machinery – Juvenile literature.
2. Siphons – Juvenile literature. 3. Handicraft –
Juvenile literature. [1. Pumping machinery – Experiments. 2. Siphons – Experiments. 3. Experiments]
I. Lindblom, Steven. II. Title. III. Series:
Boston. Children's Museum. Children's Museum
activity book.
TJ903.Z8   621.6   80-29462

ISBN 0-316-98877-4 (pbk.)

10 9 8 7 6 5 4

Published simultaneously in Canada
by Little, Brown & Company (Canada) Limited

PRINTED IN THE UNITED STATES OF AMERICA

To the children of the D Street Multi-Service Center
in South Boston, and those of the Roxbury Boys' Club
who had great fun playing with water pumps. May their
children some day in the future share in the same explorations.

INTRODUCTION

Moving liquids from one point to another may not seem important when you first think about it, yet our very life depends on this process. Our hearts are continually pumping blood through our bodies. Water is necessary for our survival. Today, moving it from lakes or rivers to buildings in cities requires pumps. Other important systems depend on specially designed pumps for their functioning. How gasoline is delivered to the car's engine is one example. In each of these situations, the pump is different, but all operate on similar principles.

By playing around with water and some common materials you can begin to understand these principles and how such things as pumps work. It is best to start with simple experiments. Gradually you can make some working models that are based on these simple experiments. As a result, you will not only see but also get a feeling for how something works.

On the following pages there are descriptions of all sorts of water devices. There are enough instructions to get you started. Sometimes you may have trouble getting the result mentioned in the book. This is an excellent opportunity to act like a real detective and try to track down that small detail that may make the difference between the experiment's working or not working. There are also lots of questions to make you think about what is happening in each system.

Once you have done all of the activities in this book, there is still plenty to discover and invent. This book will show you some of the possibilities and start you out.

SIPHONING

If you have to remove water from an aquarium, you don't just pour it out. It's a lot easier to place a tube in the water and siphon it into a bucket.

This technique for moving water from one container to another seems simple. All you do is put the tube in the water, suck at one end, and the water starts flowing. But is it that simple?

Have you ever siphoned water? Get yourself a piece of tubing and experiment with the following kind of arrangement. This can be purchased at either a hardware store or an aquarium supply house.

Here are some questions to start your experimenting.

Once the water starts flowing, does it make any difference if you move the end of the tubing in and out of the bucket?

What happens when you raise the bucket higher than the jar?

Which way will the water flow?

Can you make the water flow faster or more slowly?

Is there a way to start the siphon without sucking at the end? Look around the kitchen. You may have something like a baster. How could you use this with the tubing to get the siphon started?

Having experimented with the tubing in several ways, you should discover some important facts.

First, when the flow of water is starting, the end of the tubing has to be below the level of the water in the jar, or else the water won't flow from the jar to the bucket.

Second, if you lift the bucket higher than the jar while the water is flowing, the water will move in the opposite direction, back to the jar.

In siphoning, water moves downward, and it will continue to do so until the container is empty or the levels in the two containers are the same.

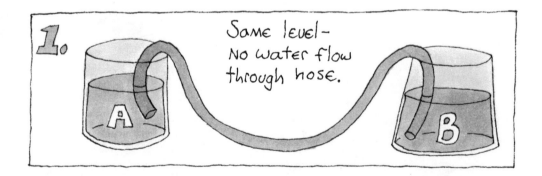

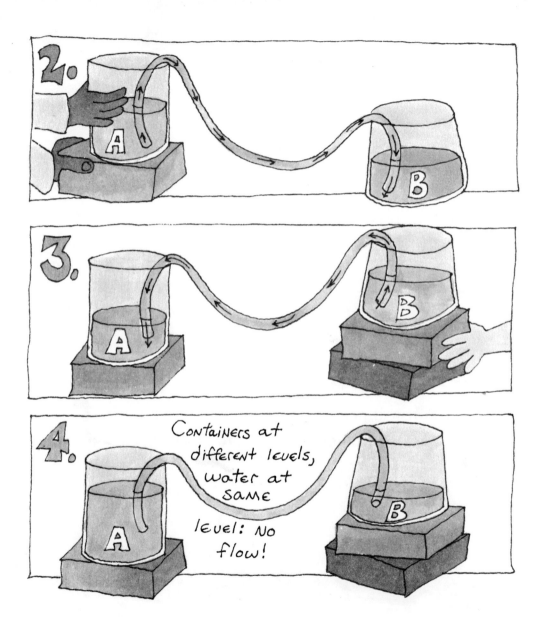

The Siphon Bottle: A Multipurpose Device

Usually in siphoning you end up with a mouthful of water when trying to get started. There are ways of overcoming this problem. One such arrangement is the siphon bottle. It is not only useful in siphoning, but it also can be made into all sorts of water devices. At the same time, it will help you understand some interesting properties of air and water.

As shown in the drawing, the two pieces of tubing are held in place by a stopper.

You will need two pieces of flexible tubing.

The length does not have to be exactly as shown.

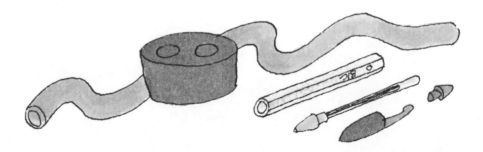

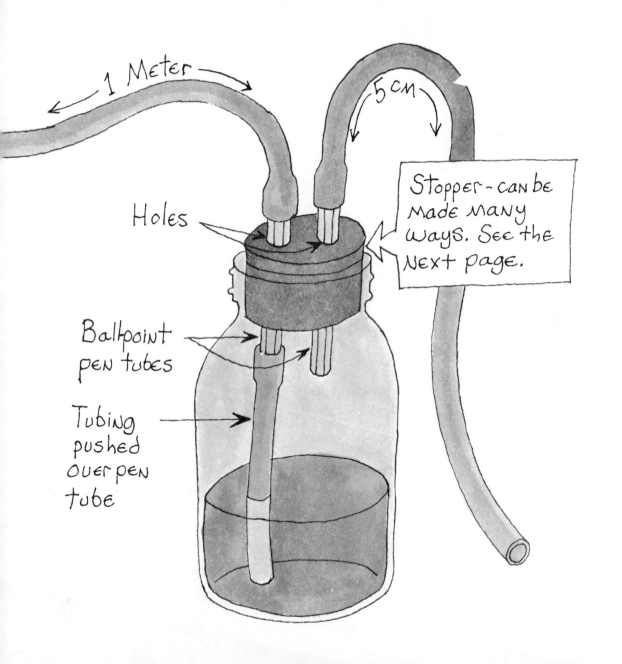

RUBBER BALL

Don't force the ball too hard or you'll have a handful of broken glass!

STOPPERS

PLASTIC BAG

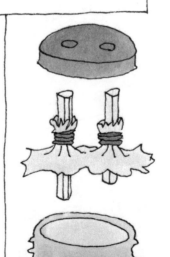

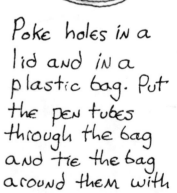

Poke holes in a lid and in a plastic bag. Put the pen tubes through the bag and tie the bag around them with rubber bands.

The stopper can be made from a variety of things, such as a sponge rubber ball, a cork from a thermos, a rubber stopper, or a plastic bag.

Since rubber balls and cork come in only one or two sizes, find a jar in which either will fit snugly. Next, with the help of an adult, drill two holes a little smaller than the diameter of the tubing. If you are using thick tubing, it is best to use two pieces of rigid tubing such as the outer part of a ball-point pen for the part that goes through the stopper. The thick flexible tubing may be too difficult to push through the holes.

If you are using a small ball and small-diameter tubing, you can poke the tubing through the ball, first using a nail or screwdriver to make a hole.

You can also use a plastic bag. This doesn't work as well as the cork or ball, but if you make sure there is a tight fit around the tubing and the lid, it will work for most of the activities in this book.

Messing Around with the Siphon Bottle

Having assembled the bottle, you can immediately put it to use. With the longest piece of tubing in a bucket of water, try sucking on the shorter piece of tubing and see if you can get water to come into the bottle. This arrangement is similar in its operation to the single piece of tubing, but you can do much more with it. Play around with the bottle and a bucket of water. Try all sorts of ways of using the tubing to get the water into or out of the bottle. Also, place the bottle in different positions, hold it upside down, on its side, high above the bucket. Watch the flow of water carefully and note whether it comes out quickly or slowly.

Then consider the following questions:

Can you get the water to flow into the bottle by itself without continually sucking?

What happens when you raise or lower the bottle as water is coming into it?

Turn the bottle upside down with the water in it.

Can you get the water to flow more quickly or slowly out of the bottle?

By closing off one of the tubes with your finger, can you stop and start the flow of water?

Can you get the water to flow out of the bottle if one of the tubes is closed off?

If you have attempted to find answers to the above questions, you might have noticed this: water will flow from one container to another only when the two water levels are different. In the closed container, air has to go out in order for water to come into the bottle, and when the water goes back out, air comes in.

PUSHING WATER UPWARD — FIRE EXTINGUISHERS

As already mentioned, the water in a siphon is always moving downward. The advantage to a siphon bottle is that the water can be moved into or out of the bottle depending on whether you are blowing or sucking one of the tubes. In fact, if you blow hard, you can not only move the water upward, but even have it squirt out of the bottle. If you haven't tried this yet, fill a bottle with water and see how far sideways and upward you can make the water squirt.

In this way, you can make the siphon bottle into something like a water pistol or fire extinguisher. But blowing with your lungs like this can become tiring. An easier technique is to have an air reservoir that, when squeezed, will push the water out. On the following pages are some suggestions for making one. Perhaps you could invent some devices yourself.

Take a dishwashing detergent bottle. Find one whose top fits the kind of tubing you are using.

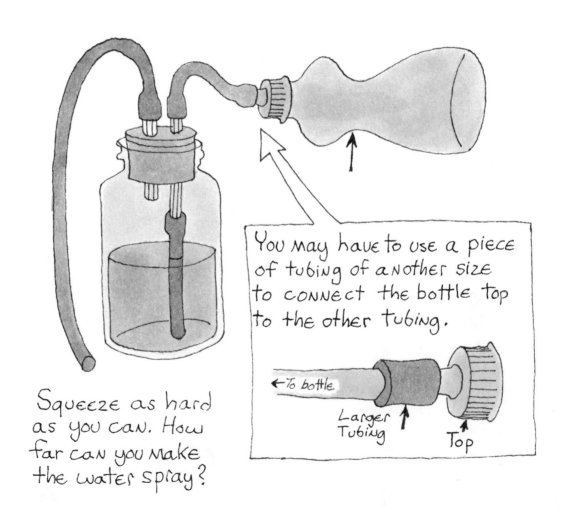

You may have to use a piece of tubing of another size to connect the bottle top to the other tubing.

← To bottle

Larger Tubing

Top

Squeeze as hard as you can. How far can you make the water spray?

Balloons can also be attached to the siphon bottles. Just remove the detergent bottle from the cap and put the balloon over it. Round balloons with narrow necks work the best.

Slip the balloon neck over the cap.

Stretch the first balloon over a pencil, then

slip the second balloon over the first.

For more pressure try a double balloon

Before attaching the balloon to the bottle, blow it up and twist the neck so the air won't come out. Then, slip it on the other part of the tubing. If you squeeze the balloon hard with both hands you can get the water to squirt out of the bottle. Try putting one balloon inside another. This will enable you to put more air in the balloon.

While playing with the balloon and siphon bottle, here are other questions to explore.

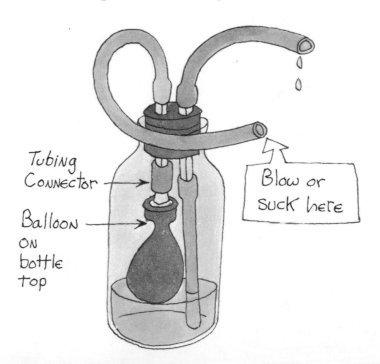

Tubing
Connector

Balloon
ON
bottle
top

Blow or
suck here

Can you blow up the balloon with air even when it is attached to the bottle?

Can you fill the balloon with water when it is attached to the bottle?

When a balloon is attached to the bottle and filled with water, what happens as you raise and lower the balloon?

Try sticking the balloon inside the bottle, as shown. What happens when you blow into or suck on the one tube?

A third source of air you could attach to the bottle is a bicycle pump. You will have to figure out a way of attaching the stem of the pump to your bottle. Tubing of a different diameter or parts of a ball-point pen may help.

Bicycle pump

Same old siphon bottle

BE CAREFUL!
   Don't pump too hard or block the outlet tube or it could be "broken glass flying through the air" time! — No fun!

Each of these situations is similar to the operation of a real fire extinguisher. The gas in the bottle on the side has been compressed so that it is under high pressure. When the valve at the top is turned, the gas pushes with great force on the liquid and sends it out through the other tube.

Compressed gas

Valve

Water

ANOTHER KIND

Soda

Acid and water

When the extinguisher is turned upside down the soda and acid mix, spraying out the water.

With the simple materials that your parents may have around their kitchen, you can make your own fire extinguisher.

You will need the following materials: dishwashing detergent bottle—a transparent one would be best—baking soda, small plastic Baggies, and vinegar.

1. Pour ½ cup vinegar into bottle.

2. Put 2-3 tbsp. of baking soda into Baggie. Don't close it.

3. Put the Baggie carefully into the bottle.

Closed

4. Screw cap on tight, making sure the value is closed.

Shake so vinegar mixes with baking soda.

When you shake this bottle, note how the sides bulge. Turn the bottle upside down and point the nozzle into a sink. Be very careful not to point it at your face or at another person. Open the valve at the top. How long does the spray last? What can you do to make it last longer? What can you do to make it shoot out farther? It would be best to do this part of your experiment outside.

This arrangement with the detergent bottle is similar to aerosol cans like the ones hair spray and spray paint come in. The drawing shows how one works.

The liquid and the gas are placed in the can together. As with the fire extinguisher on the previous page, the gas is pushing with a great deal of force. Pushing down on the knob at the top opens the tube, and the liquid comes rushing out.

Valve

Compressed gas

Can

Liquid

SPRA
FISH

MOVING WATER UP ANOTHER WAY— AIR THERMOMETERS

In all the previous experiments you pushed water up one tube by pushing air into the bottle through the other tube. If you close off one of the tubes, as shown in the drawing, is it still possible to make water rise up the other? Clamp the shorter tube with a clothespin or just stopper the end. See if you can find some way to get the water to rise.

Here are two ways you can try.

From the previous experiment we found that if the air pressure inside the bottle is increased, the water will be pushed out. One way to do this with one tube is to blow as hard as you can into the open tubing so that air is squeezed into the bottle, then quickly take your mouth away. (For this to work well, the stopper needs to be leak-proof.)

How high can you make the water rise in the tube?

Can you get any water to drain out of the tube?

There is another way of getting the same result that is much easier. Prop up one tube with a stick so that it is vertical. Then just hold the bottle with your hands for several minutes. Watch the section of the tube in the bottle carefully. If you concentrate hard, you can make the water rise.

Try this several times and see if you get the same result every time. Now, is it your brain waves making

the water rise, or something else? To see what is really happening here, and to get an even better result, find a large bowl or bucket and fill it with very warm water. Keeping one tube vertical, carefully place the bottle in this water. Wait for a few minutes and watch the bottom part of the tube in the bottle closely.

In both these situations the same thing is happening. The heat from your hands or from the bucket of warm water is causing the air to expand in the bottle. Since it is expanding, it pushes down on the water, and the only place for the water to move is up the tubing.

There are a number of variations to this arrangement. Different amounts of water inside the bottle might give different results. What about different-size bottles?

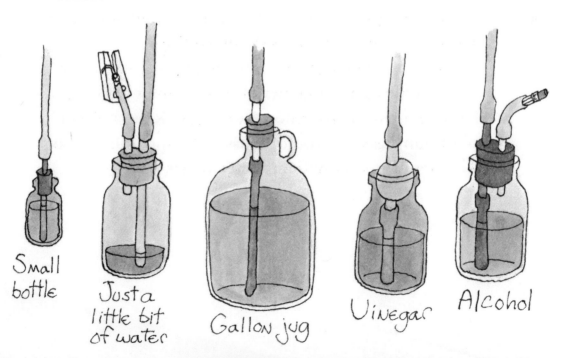

Small bottle

Just a little bit of water

Gallon jug

Vinegar

Alcohol

Try other variations, as shown in the drawing. See if you can predict what will happen.

First, try placing your hands on both bottles and waiting for a while. See if you can get the water to climb to the same height as before.

What happens when you place each bottle in a bucket of hot water?

What happens if you first place each in hot water, then in cold water?

What happens if you leave each arrangement near a window where the sun is shining?

Do other liquids give you the same results as water?

This type of arrangement is very similar to the first kind of medical thermometer. Jean Rey, a French physician, used a type of glass bulb and tube to see whether or not his patients had a fever.

MEASURING AIR PRESSURE

Several different ways to move water upward have been shown. All of these involve increasing the air pressure inside a siphon bottle. Just how much does each of these techniques raise the pressure? How do they compare to each other?

To get some relative idea, you need a measuring instrument of some kind. The siphon bottle itself can be converted into such an instrument. The most important preparation for doing this is to make sure there are no leaks around the stopper. You can check by putting the bottle under water. Close off the end of one tube and blow hard into the other. If there are leaks, bubbles will show where they are. You may have to make a new stopper arrangement to get a good tight fit.

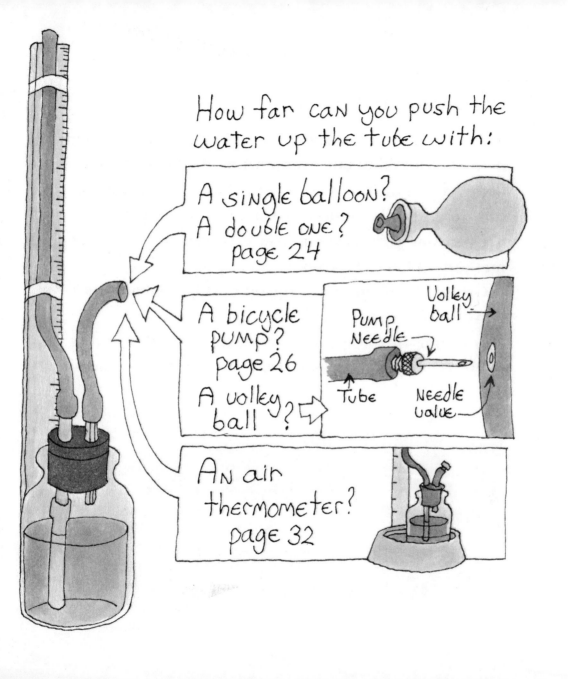

How far can you push the
water up the tube with:

A single balloon?
A double one?
    page 24

A bicycle
pump?
page 26

A volley
ball?

A air
thermometer?
page 32

Pump
Needle

Volley
ball

Tube

Needle
valve

Decreasing Air Pressure

So far, you have always been increasing the air pressure in the bottle. What takes place when the opposite happens? If you suck on one of the tubes in the bottle you can, in certain situations, decrease the air pressure. To see how this happens you can use the following method, called the Cartesian diver trick.

Get two eyedroppers or the outer tubes of ball-point pens.

Into one of these put enough water so that it just floats. It is very important that the weight be exactly

right. Put water into the other one until it sinks.

Place these in a siphon bottle full of water. Clamp or close off one of the tubes. Now you are ready for an interesting trick.

Try sucking as hard as you can on the other tube and watch what happens to the dropper at the bottom of the bottle. Blow as hard as you can and watch what happens to the dropper that is floating. If there is the

Clamp or plug the end.

Blow very hard here.

Plugged

Suck hard here.

right amount of water in each, one will rise to the top when you suck, and the other will sink when you blow hard.

The eyedropper in the bottle sinks or floats because of the changing air pressure. When you blow air into a bottle that has been completely closed off, the air at the top of the water is at a greater pressure than air outside the bottle. This pressure is also felt by the water, with the result that the air trapped in the eye-dropper is squeezed. More water enters the dropper, making it heavier, so the dropper sinks.

The opposite happens when you suck on the tubing. The air pressure decreases inside the bottle. The air inside the dropper expands, making it lighter, and therefore it starts to float.

PULLING WATER UPWARD

The siphon works by the water's moving downward. The fire extinguisher and air thermometer work when water is pushed out of the container or up the tube. What happens when water is pulled instead of pushed? An everyday example of this effect happens when you use a drinking straw to drink soda. Ordinarily, you use a straw to pull up the soda, but what would happen if you had a very long straw? Could you still pull the soda up if you had a straw or tubing two, three, or four meters long?

You could try this by using one tube of the siphon bottle. Try to make one tube as long as possible. Stand on a chair with the bottle on the floor and see how high up you can suck the water. After you have done this several times, close off the other tube and make sure the stopper doesn't leak. Can you suck the water as high with this arrangement?

PULLING WATER UPHILL— SUCTION PUMPS

Balloons were used to push water out of the siphon bottle. Can they be used in some way to pull water out?

The following drawing shows how a piece of balloon attached to a funnel can pull water up. If further additions are made, it can be made into a suction pump.

If you move the balloon up and down on the funnel, you will find that water in the tube will move up and down in the tubing. To keep the water in the funnel,

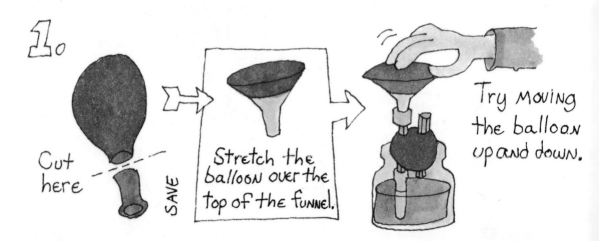

1.

Cut here

SAVE

Stretch the balloon over the top of the funnel.

Try moving the balloon up and down.

you will need a valve. (This can easily be made by using a piece of balloon.) Valves are a very important part of the pump. Without them it would not be possible to move the water upward. To complete the pump you need a place for the water to leave the funnel. A hole on the side of the funnel has to be made, tubing must be placed in this hole, and another balloon valve

Put the balloon neck on a piece of tubing and force it into the funnel.

Put another balloon valve and tube through a hole in the funnel.

put on the end of this. Then you can pump water up short distances by pulling and pushing on the balloon.

To operate, push down on balloon, then pull up. It will take several pump strokes to get the water moving.

This type of pump is similar to ones found in older automobiles, which moved the gasoline from the tank to the carburetor. It is also somewhat like the most important pump of all, the human heart.

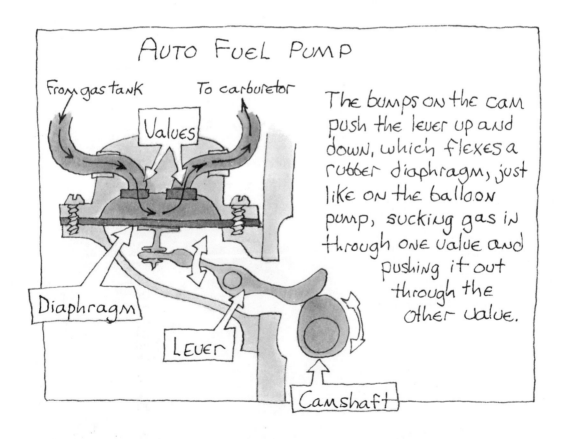

AUTO FUEL PUMP

From gas tank

To carburetor

Valves

Diaphragm

Lever

Camshaft

The bumps on the cam push the lever up and down, which flexes a rubber diaphragm, just like on the balloon pump, sucking gas in through one valve and pushing it out through the other valve.

The valves in the heart are like the pieces of balloon in the suction pump. They are made of tissue that lets blood move in one direction only. The blood is pumped by the squeezing action of the muscles of the heart.

The following drawing shows how the heart works.

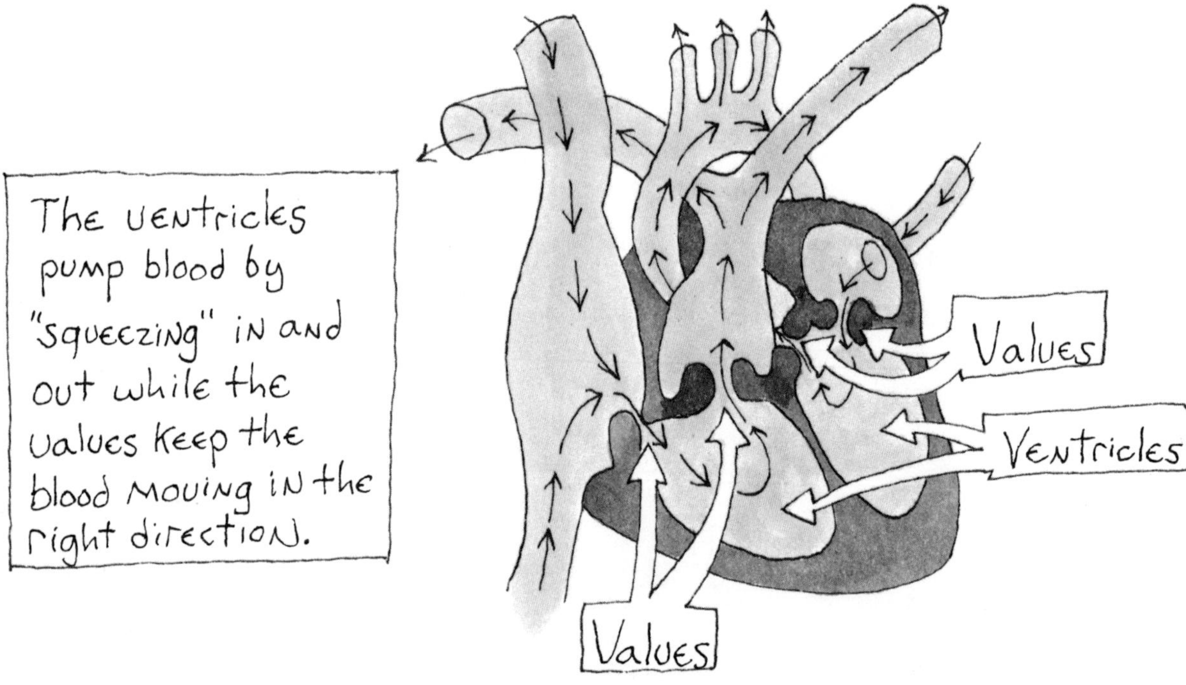

The ventricles pump blood by "squeezing" in and out while the valves keep the blood moving in the right direction.

Values

Values

Ventricles

Values

OTHER KINDS OF PUMPS

The baster in your parents' kitchen is a very simple pump. However, it is not very efficient as it is. You have to squeeze the bulb, let the liquid come up in the tube, take the full baster out of the container, then squeeze the liquid into another container. Here is a way of making a continually operating pump using the baster.

   1. Cut a small hole on the side of the baster near the top. Make it about 2 cm. wide.

2. Get a sausage-shaped balloon and make a small slit so that it can be slid on the tube as shown. This is one valve.

3. Put a marble inside the tube. This will be your other valve.

4. Put the rubber bulb on the tube.

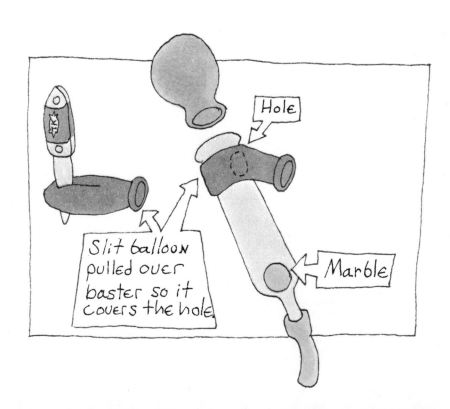

How to operate:

Squeeze the bulb several times. If your valves are working properly, water should rise up the tube and squirt out the piece of balloon. Make sure the balloon covers the entire hole in the baster.

You can attach pieces of tubing to the end of the baster and experiment to see how high you can pull the water up the tube.

The same baster can be modified in another way and be made into a force pump, one of the most common types of pumps.

Wood dowel ½ inch (1.5 cm) thick

Bicycle tire patch

Trim patch so it fits snugly in the baster.

Marble valve

Water

How to operate:

Pumps like these have to be primed first. This means that you put water into the top part of the pump. Then you move the plunger-piston up and down. The water helps you get a good seal around the valves so that on the upstroke you will have good suction to pull the water up the tubing from the bucket.

Here, also, you can test your pump and see how strong it is by attaching tubing to the narrow end of the baster. Will the pump still pull water up when the pump is 1, 2, or 3 meters above the water level in the bucket?

PULLING WATER UPWARD USING HEAT

In a previous section it was shown how heat could be used to push water upward. The result was a type of thermometer. Heat also can be used to pull water upward, and another kind of thermometer is based on this idea.

Many years ago, at the beginning of the seventeenth century, various attempts were made to measure hotness and coldness. Galileo was one of the first to make a device to do this. He took a glass vial about the size of an egg and attached a tube to it.

If Galileo had wanted to measure the temperature of a sick person, he would have had the person place his or her hands on the bottle. This bottle was full of air, and the end of the tubing was sitting in another bottle of water. Try the same arrangement with the siphon bottle and watch the end of the tubing carefully. Hold the bottle for several minutes. Keeping the end

of the tubing in the water, take your hands off the bottle and watch what happens in the tubing. Measure how far up the tubing the water rises.

Have other people hold the bottle for the same amount of time. Let the bottle sit without holding it for the same amount of time as before. Does the water rise the same amount as when you held the bottle?

This arrangement that Galileo developed was not satisfactory because the results obtained were not consistent. One reason was that the weather had an effect on it.

THE BEGINNINGS OF
THE STEAM ENGINE

Although Galileo's "thermoscope" did not prove to be useful, it produced an interesting result. Remember that after cooling, the water in the bottle rose a few inches up the tube. Since only your hands were used to heat the bottle, what would happen if the bottle were heated much more? Would much more water be pulled up the bottle? You can try the following and see what happens.

Put the bottle into bucket of hot water. Be careful with hot water!

Hot water →

← Cold water

Pouring hot water onto the bottle will help this happen more quickly. After the bubbles have stopped coming out of the tube in bottle B, take the bottle out of the bucket. Use heavy rubber gloves or tongs to do this. Keep the tubing in the other bottle. Let bottle A cool. If you have a good seal at the stopper, water should rise up the tubing.

What is the highest point to which you can get the bottle to pull water up when the water is cooling?

What would happen if you used a larger bottle?

What would happen if you used hotter water? Have an adult help you with this. It may be safer, too, to use a tin can to pull up the water.

This technique for cooling a hot chamber was investigated in the seventeenth century. However, instead of heating the air in a chamber, hot steam was placed inside of it. When hot steam is cooled inside a space, the same results are produced that you got when you took the hot bottle out of the bucket.

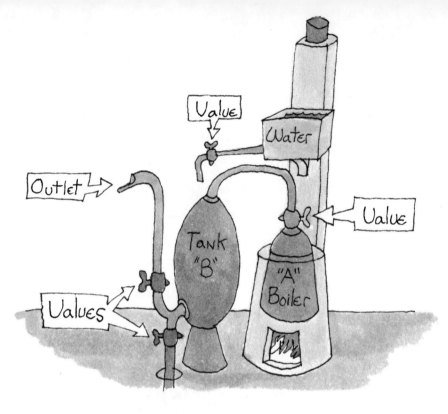

One of the first heat engines that worked like this was invented by an English engineer named Thomas Savery.

Steam was made in a special container. It was allowed to enter chamber B by way of a valve.

Cold water flowed over container B. This contact resulted in a reduced pressure, just as the cooling off in the bottle resulted in a reduced pressure. The water came up the pipe to container B. Then steam was used to push the water out of B to a higher point.

In this manner water was pumped out of coal mines in England. Not long after the use of this engine, other engineers made improvements. Eventually, other steam engines resulted.

Force Pump

Early Steam Engine

FURTHER EXPLORATIONS

As you have seen, the siphon bottle can be a very versatile device. This book has mentioned only a few ways of making various kinds of pumps. You could use the siphon bottle to study how pressure in different kinds of water systems varies. By connecting several siphon bottles together, you could see how water movement happens in complex systems. By playing around with the siphon bottle, you could also come up with your own inventions, so hang on to your tubing and bottle and see what you can discover.

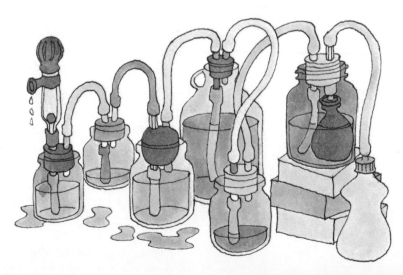